PEOPLES of NORTH AMERICA

Shawnee

VALERIE BODDEN

CREATIVE EDUCATION · CREATIVE PAPERBACKS

Published by Creative Education and Creative Paperbacks
P.O. Box 227, Mankato, Minnesota 56002
Creative Education and Creative Paperbacks
are imprints of The Creative Company
www.thecreativecompany.us

Design and production by Christine Vanderbeek
Art direction by Rita Marshall
Printed in China

Photographs by Alamy (The Artchives, Yvette Cardozo, Danita Delimont, Glasshouse Images,
IllustratedHistory, Science History Images), Creative Commons Wikimedia (George Caleb
Bingham/Washington University, St. Louis; George Catlin), Dreamstime (Seth Johnson,
Mikael Males, Pam Wallis), Getty Images (Bettmann, Charles Phelps Cushing/ClassicStock,
Chicago History Museum/Archive Photos, Nativestock.com/Marilyn Angel Wynn, Marilyn
Angel Wynn), iStockphoto (andipantz, Bikemech, ivan-96), Shutterstock (SMIRNOVA IRINA,
Robert L Kothenbeutel, Alex Leo, MarkVanDykePhotography, OHishiapply, outdoorimages,
Susilyn, Transia Design, Michiel de Wit), Smithsonian Institution (Department of Anthropology,
Smithsonian Institution/National Museum of the American Indian), SuperStock (Tony Linck)

Library of Congress Cataloging-in-Publication Data
Names: Bodden, Valerie, author.
Title: Shawnee / Valerie Bodden.
Series: Peoples of North America.
Includes bibliographical references and index.
Summary: A history of the people and events that influenced the North American Indian tribe
known as the Shawnee, including chief Tecumseh and conflicts such as Little Turtle's War.
Identifiers: LCCN 2017044005 / ISBN 978-1-60818-968-7 (hardcover) /
ISBN 978-1-62832-595-9 (pbk) / ISBN 978-1-64000-069-8 (eBook)
Subjects: LCSH: Shawnee Indians—History—Juvenile literature.
Classification: LCC E99.S35 B64 2018 / DDC 974.004/97317—dc23

CCSS: RI.5.1, 2, 3, 5, 6, 8, 9; RH.6–8.4, 5, 6, 7, 8, 9

First Edition HC 9 8 7 6 5 4 3 2 1
First Edition PBK 9 8 7 6 5 4 3 2 1

PEOPLES of NORTH AMERICA

Shawnee

VALERIE BODDEN

CREATIVE EDUCATION • CREATIVE PAPERBACKS

Table of Contents

The Shawnee chief Tecumseh (on page 3);
drummers at an annual powwow in Ohio
(pictured here).

The Shawnee Indians have been referred to as "the greatest travelers in America." At different times in their history, they have resided in various regions of the eastern United States. They roamed the peaks of the Appalachian Mountains, the lands of the Southeast, and the hills and valleys of the Ohio River Valley. Nearly everywhere they moved, though, they were always surrounded by thick forests. Deer, elk, bears, mountain lions, and turkeys made their homes in the woodlands. In places, the trees opened to reveal patches of long prairie grasses where bison grazed or low marshes that gave shelter to waterfowl. Fast-flowing streams and lazy rivers wound through the landscape. These waters held a wealth of pike, bass, and other fish. As the Shawnee traveled, they adapted to a wide range of climates, from the hot, humid summers of the Southeast to the icy winter blizzards of the Ohio Valley. No matter where they went, they trusted the land would provide all they needed.

The name "Shawnee" comes from an Algonquian word meaning "southerners." This may be because the Shawnee generally lived south of other Algonquian-speaking peoples. As they moved across eastern North America, the Shawnee fought hard against the French, British, and American settlers who tried to lay claim to their lands. Eventually, they were forced to move west to Indian Territory, in present-day Oklahoma, where they struggled to retain their culture and traditions. That struggle continues today.

THE SHAWNEE RANGED THROUGH THE WOODED MOUNTAINS OF PRESENT-DAY APPALACHIA.

· SHAWNEE ·

Great Travelers

PEOPLES *of* NORTH AMERICA

According to author Allan W. Eckert, "Unlike virtually all the other [American Indian] tribes, which sank their roots in a specified territory and remained there, the Shawnee were astonishingly **NOMADIC**—traveling, warring, moving, pausing, and then traveling again." Because they traveled so widely and often broke into separate groups, the history of the Shawnee is difficult to trace. **ANTHROPOLOGISTS**, historians, and the Shawnee people disagree about the location of the original Shawnee homeland. Shawnee oral history recounts a time when the people lived in Mexico, then traveled to Florida and Georgia before moving north. However, the Shawnee language belongs to the Algonquian language family—which also includes the languages of the Delaware, Miami, Kickapoo, Illinois, Sauk, and Fox Indians. As a result, many anthropologists believe the Shawnee are descended from Algonquin peoples who originally lived in Canada and slowly migrated south.

The Shawnee's ancestors may have been among the first Algonquins to move south. These early Algonquin travelers eventually settled along the Ohio River in the present-day states of Ohio, West Virginia, and Kentucky. Anthropologists refer to the culture that flourished in this region from about A.D. 1000 to 1650 as

SOME OF THE FIRST EUROPEAN-PERSPECTIVE DRAWINGS OF AMERICAN INDIANS WERE DONE IN THE 1580S BY ENGLISHMAN JOHN WHITE.

the Fort Ancient culture. The Fort Ancient people lived in villages along riverbanks. They farmed, fished, and hunted.

By about 1630, Fort Ancient societies began to leave the lands that had been their home for more than 600 years. They may have been pushed off the land by attacks from the Iroquois to the east. In addition, warfare between the Iroquois and the Susquehannock may have prevented European trade goods from reaching the Ohio River Valley. This would have caused hardships among American Indians who had grown dependent on such goods. Some Fort Ancient people moved southeast or northwest to be closer to traders. Others may have been driven out of the area by slavers who invaded the territory and carried off American Indian captives. European diseases, such as smallpox and influenza, may also have reached the Ohio River Valley at this time. Because the Indians had never encountered these diseases before, they had no immunity to them. Many died.

Traveling on foot, without wagons or **TRAVOIS**, the Fort Ancient people moved as small villages or family bands. Women carried the family's belongings, while men carried weapons for protection as well as to shoot game along the way. The bands

⤙⟐⟐ **WHISTLE WHILE YOU HUNT** ⟐⟐⤚ *In addition to imitating animal sounds to sneak up on prey, the Shawnee used bird whistles and other animal calls to communicate while hunting. As children, the Shawnee learned a special whistled code for their names. Each syllable had its own note. Settlers sometimes remarked on the sweet bird calls, never realizing they were made by Shawnee hidden nearby. Others learned of the Shawnee's unique method of communication and became terrified whenever they heard birdsong in the forest.*

covered only a few miles a day. They remained in camps for weeks
or months at a time before moving on.

By 1680, no Fort Ancient villages remained in the Ohio
Valley. The Shawnee people spread across parts of New York,
Pennsylvania, Maryland, Virginia, South Carolina, Georgia,
Alabama, Kentucky, and Illinois. Because they had a reputation
as fierce fighters, many were invited to settle among other tribes,
such as the Creek and Cherokee. In return for protection, these
tribes provided the Shawnee with lands for hunting and farming.
Other allies throughout Shawnee history included the Delaware,
Mingo, Huron, Erie, and Miami. Their fiercest enemies were the
Iroquois of the Northeast. In the Southeast, the Shawnee battled
the Catawba and Chickasaw and completely displaced the Westo
peoples. Those Shawnee who moved west toward the Mississippi
River faced off against the Osage and Caddo.

The Shawnee remained dispersed across eastern North
America until the 1720s and '30s, when many moved back to the
Ohio River Valley. There, the Wyandot people granted them land
on which to establish new villages. A few scattered Shawnee bands
remained in Virginia, Alabama, and Kentucky.

⇒ **THE TRADITIONAL LOOK** ⇐ *Traditionally, Shawnee women made clothing from deerskin. In the summer, men wore only breechcloths. Women wore loose shirts and wrap skirts. In the winter, both men and women wore leggings, shirts, and fur cloaks. Most Shawnee clothing included decorations of dyed porcupine quills, beads, and feathers. Men often wore nose rings and earrings. They donned headbands of animal fur and feathers for ceremonies. Women wore their long hair in two buns at the side of the head. Later, many Shawnee adopted the clothing of Europeans or Americans.*

Although the Shawnee may have started out as a united tribe, by the 1700s, they were split into five divisions, or groups, known as septs. Each sept governed itself. Together, the five septs formed a loose Shawnee **CONFEDERACY** that might come together for significant decisions or warfare. In addition, each division held certain responsibilities within the overall tribe. The Chillicothe and Thawekila divisions took charge of political matters. The Shawnee principal chief usually came from one of these two septs. The Mekoche provided healers and medicine. The Pekowi oversaw religious ceremonies, and the Kispoko prepared the tribe for warfare. A Shawnee child belonged to the same division as his or her father.

Like sept membership, clan membership was also inherited from the father. The Shawnee may have originally recognized more than 30 clans. But by the 1800s, only 12 clans remained. Each clan was named after an animal or plant: Snake, Turtle, Raccoon, Turkey, Hawk, Deer, Bear, Wolf, Panther, Elk, Buffalo, and Tree. Members of a clan were said to share characteristics with the animal or plant of their clan name. A Shawnee could not marry someone from the same clan.

Members of various divisions and clans lived together in

villages during the summer months. Shawnee villages generally housed 20 to 300 people. Palisades, or tall fences made of posts with sharpened tops, surrounded the villages for protection. At the center of each village was a council house called a *msikame-kwi*. This log structure measured up to 150 feet (45.7 m) long and 30 feet (9.1 m) wide. The Shawnee used the building for religious and political gatherings. When under attack, villagers fled into the council house for safety.

Shawnee families lived in square or oblong wigwams made of a frame of saplings with a sloped roof. Sheets of bark or animal skins covered the frame to keep the home warm and dry, even in winter. The structure had no windows, but a hole in the center of the roof allowed smoke from the cooking fire inside to escape.

In the fall and winter, the Shawnee left their villages to hunt in small groups. While on the hunt, they built smaller, dome-shaped versions of their wigwams. Each structure might hold only one or two people. Building materials were abundant in the woodlands of eastern North America. As a result, the Shawnee did not bring their homes with them when they moved, unlike many of the nomadic Indians of the western plains. It was faster and easier to simply abandon the structures. When they reached a new hunting camp, the women built a new home.

Meat from the hunt—which included elk, deer, bear, and turkey—provided for much of the Shawnee's nutritional needs. Meat was generally eaten roasted, boiled, or fried in bear grease. Some meat was dried for later use. In addition to hunting, the Shawnee fished, farmed, and gathered wild plants. The Shawnee found that the land provided all they needed. They felt a deep connection to it. And they were willing to defend it from any who encroached.

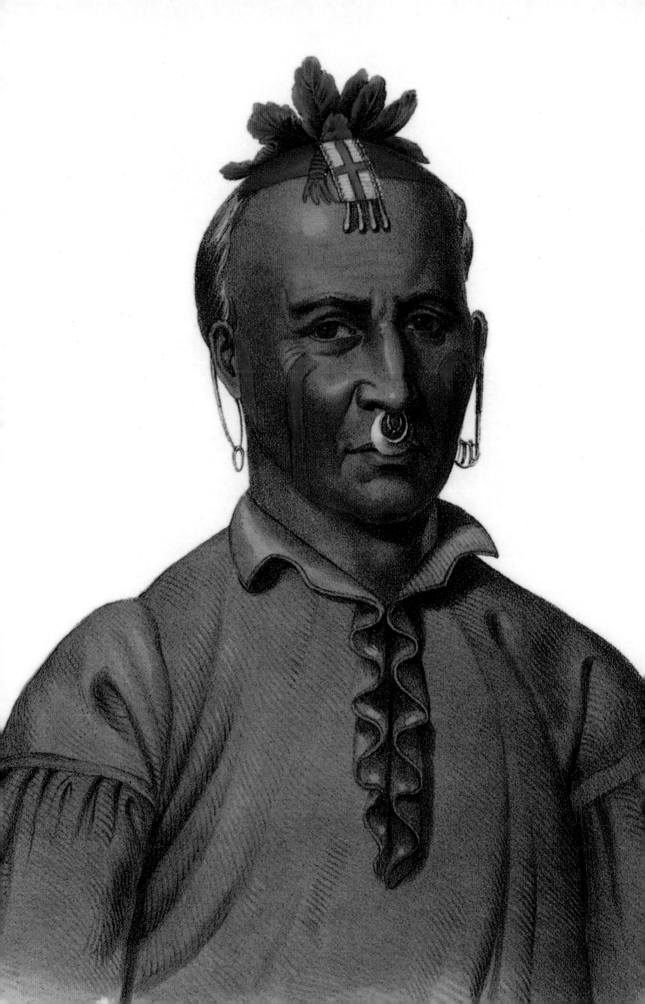

Because the Shawnee were spread across such a vast region, their most important social group was the village. Each level of society—the village, the sept, and the tribe—was led by two chiefs: a peace chief and a war chief. Peace, or civil, chiefs oversaw day-to-day matters and organized religious rituals. This position was generally passed down from father to son.

The position of war chief was earned rather than inherited. A war chief first had to show skill and bravery in battle by leading at least four raids. He had to return from each raid with enemy **SCALPS**, and he couldn't lose any of his own men during the fighting. The war chief took over leadership during times of war but returned leadership to the peace chief once the war had ended. At times, the same man held both the war and peace chief positions.

Both the peace and war chiefs were guided by a council of elders. The council offered advice to the chief. Usually, the chief did not make a decision until there was a **CONSENSUS**. Once a decision was made, however, the council and chiefs had no way to enforce it. Those who chose not to go along with a decision generally were not forced to do so.

At the village level, women also served in positions of authority. In

THE SHAWNEE WAR CHIEF KISHKALWA LED MANY SUCCESSFUL SHAWNEE BATTLES IN THE LATE 1700S AND EARLY 1800S.

addition to the male war and peace chiefs, many villages recognized separate female war and peace chiefs. Often, these women were the mothers or relatives of the male chiefs. Female chiefs oversaw women's issues, including when to plant crops or hold certain feasts. The female peace chief might try to prevent the people from going to war. After a war, she could spare the lives of captives. Female war chiefs helped with preparations for warfare. Women were sometimes allowed to sit on the village council as well because, as one Shawnee man said, "Some women were wiser than some men."

Shawnee life changed with the seasons. In the spring, men cleared the fields. Then the women planted them. The Shawnee's most important crop was sweet corn. They planted several varieties, including red, dark blue, and white. Other crops included beans, squash, pumpkins, sunflowers, and, in the south, sweet potatoes. Although each family owned its own field, the women worked together as they planted and tended crops. Throughout the summer, the women also gathered herbs, wild potatoes and onions, nuts, berries, cherries, persimmons, and other wild plants. They collected honey from beehives as well.

Men might have hunted locally as needed during the summer. But the biggest hunt took place in the fall and winter, after the women had harvested the crops. Then, the village broke up into smaller family groups, which set out on hunting trips for two to three months. Men hunted deer, elk, bears, turkeys, and bison during the winter hunt. They often disguised themselves as animals and imitated animal sounds to sneak up on their prey. Once they were close enough, they shot the animal with an arrow or clubbed it over the head. In January, the men trapped smaller

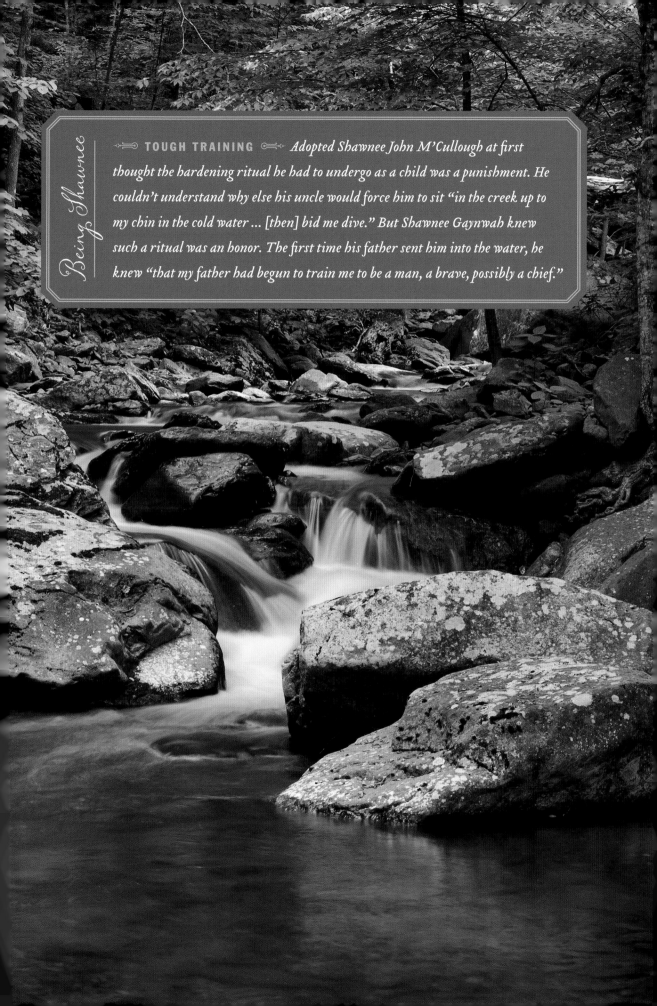

Being Shawnee

❧ **TOUGH TRAINING** ❧ *Adopted Shawnee John M'Cullough at first thought the hardening ritual he had to undergo as a child was a punishment. He couldn't understand why else his uncle would force him to sit "in the creek up to my chin in the cold water ... [then] bid me dive." But Shawnee Gaynwah knew such a ritual was an honor. The first time his father sent him into the water, he knew "that my father had begun to train me to be a man, a brave, possibly a chief."*

fur-bearing animals. They could trade the pelts of these animals for European goods. In February, the women tapped maple trees to collect sap for maple syrup. By March, the people began to return to their villages for a new season of planting.

QUATAWAPEA, ALSO KNOWN AS COLONEL LEWIS, LED SHAWNEE WARRIORS TO HELP THE AMERICANS IN THE WAR OF 1812.

In addition to hunting, Shawnee men were expected to serve as warriors. The council decided when the people should go to war. Its decision was announced by the war chief. The war chief then sent a red tomahawk to nearby Shawnee and allied villages. The tomahawk served as an invitation to join the war party.

Before going into battle, the Shawnee took part in a war dance. Warriors drank a special beverage and **FASTED**. Then they set out, singing and brandishing war clubs, bows and arrows, and guns obtained through trade. A **SHAMAN** accompanied each war party. The shaman offered guidance and treated the injured. As they neared the enemy, young warriors were sent to hunt 12 deer. (Twelve represented the number of laws given to the Shawnee by their creator.) The men feasted on the deer as they listened to a speech by the war chief. Then they attacked.

After the battle, the men marched back to their villages. The war chief sent a messenger ahead of the war party to inform the female peace chief of their return. As they approached the village, the warriors whooped and shot off their guns, holding up a pole hung with the scalps they had taken. Prisoners were beaten as they marched into town and then turned over to the female peace chief. Some had their faces painted black, which signaled they were to be executed. Only the female peace chief had the power to change their sentence. Some captives were adopted into Shawnee families, sometimes to replace a family member who had died.

A Shawnee family generally consisted of a mother, a father, and their children. Shawnee babies were born in a small hut. Newborns remained there with their mothers for the first 10 days

of life. After this, they were named during a special ceremony. Every morning, babies were dipped into a cold stream or a snowbank. This was thought to toughen them up. Babies spent most of the day in a **CRADLEBOARD** until they were old enough to sit on their own.

As they grew up, Shawnee children were taught by their parents, grandparents, and other elders. Girls learned to farm, care for children, weave baskets, make clothes, and take care of other household chores. Boys learned to use bows and arrows by shooting at a rolling hoop. Around age nine, boys had to undergo another hardening ritual that involved diving into cold water. Around the age of 10 or 12, a young boy was sent into the woods alone. He couldn't come back to the village until he had killed an animal to eat.

⊶⇒ PAYING FOR CRIMES ⇐⊷ *In most cases, Shawnee chiefs and councils had little to do with enforcing laws. Instead, the person who had been wronged took care of the matter him- or herself. If someone had committed murder, for example, the victim's family could demand payment. The payment was twice as high for a female victim as for a male, since women could have children. At times, the family of the victim might kill the murderer instead of seeking payment. A person who had stolen might face a public beating.*

At about the same age—or sometimes even younger—boys and girls were sent on a vision quest. The child went alone into the woods to pray and fast. They hoped to encounter their guardian spirit. This spirit, which usually took the form of an animal, would watch over them and give them special powers.

The Shawnee believed spirits were present in all objects. They worshiped several gods. The Shawnee believed they had been created by a goddess called Our Grandmother. Other powerful spirits included fire, water, eagles, and the four winds.

The people appealed to the spirits through special ceremonies. The most important were the spring and fall Bread Dances. During the spring Bread Dance, the Shawnee honored women's role in farming and prayed for blessings on the harvest. At the fall Bread Dance, the people gave thanks for the harvest and honored men's position as hunters.

SHAWNEE SHAMANS HAD A REPUTATION AMONG NEIGHBORING TRIBES AS BEING ESPECIALLY POWERFUL.

The first European explorers arrived in North America in the early 1500s. They quickly began to explore and expand. Although the first recorded contact between Europeans and the Shawnee did not occur until the mid-1600s, the Shawnee likely met Spanish and French explorers and traders before then. They also obtained European goods through trade with other American Indian peoples. In the 1660s and '70s, French trappers and traders described encounters with the Shawnee in Tennessee and South Carolina. In 1673, Indian guides told French missionary Jacques Marquette that the Ohio River flowed from the east, "where dwell the people called Chaouanons [Shawnee] in so great numbers that in one district there are as many as 23 villages, and 15 in another."

The Shawnee soon met the British as well. French and British traders competed for the Shawnee's business. For their part, the Shawnee traded and allied with whichever Europeans gave them the best deal and treated them the most fairly. This often varied by region. In return for furs and hides, the Shawnee received glass beads, ribbons, pots, blankets, guns, and rum. Although they readily traded with the foreigners, the Shawnee were wary of European expansion onto their lands. Because they lived as nomadic hunters during the winter, the Shawnee needed large territories in which to find game.

FATHER JACQUES MARQUETTE WAS DEDICATED TO EDUCATING AMERICAN INDIANS ON BEHALF OF THE CATHOLIC CHURCH.

By the 1720s, European settlements had begun to push the Shawnee, who had moved east in the late 1600s, back toward the Ohio River Valley. Their return to this region placed the Shawnee on land that both the French and British wanted. In 1754, the conflict between Britain and France erupted into the **FRENCH AND INDIAN WAR**. The Shawnee did not feel great loyalty toward either nation. But several of their Indian allies had joined the French. In addition, the Shawnee believed that the French were more likely than the British to grant them their land and independence. This belief was strengthened in 1755, when British general Edward Braddock announced that if Britain won the war, "No savage should inherit the land." As a result, the Shawnee allied themselves with the French.

Shawnee war parties traveled through British settlements in Pennsylvania and Virginia, destroying homes, killing settlers, and taking captives. In conflicts with British forces, the Shawnee and other Indians fought from the cover of trees, firing at British soldiers who lined up in the open. But early victories by the French and their Indian allies didn't last. The French and Indian War ended with French defeat in 1763. The peace agreement signed at the end of the war gave all French lands in North America east of the Mississippi River to the British. French lands west of the Mississippi went to Spain. With no voice in the peace negotiations, the Shawnee soon faced a flood of settlers on their land.

In 1763, Shawnee chiefs Hokolesqua (also known as Cornstalk) and Pucksinwah allied with the Ottawa and other Indians against the British in what became known as Pontiac's Rebellion. After inflicting damage on British forts and settlements and killing hundreds of soldiers and civilians, the Indians were invited to Fort Pitt in the spring of 1763. There the British intentionally gave them blankets infested with smallpox. By the next summer, ravaged by

Being Shawnee

⇥ THE PANTHER ⇤ Born into the Panther clan in 1768, Tecumseh's name meant "the panther passing across." As a child, he fled his village with his family after American settlers burned their home and fields. Tecumseh's father and two of his brothers were killed in fights against British and American forces. When Tecumseh became a war chief, both Indians and whites took note of his courage and speaking abilities. Territorial governor WILLIAM HENRY HARRISON called Tecumseh "one of those uncommon geniuses which spring up occasionally to produce revolutions and overturn the established order of things."

disease and short on supplies, the Shawnee and other Indians were forced to surrender. At peace talks, the British warned, "We now surround you…. It is therefore in our power totally to extirpate [destroy] you from being a people."

Despite such threats, the British issued the Royal Proclamation of 1763. This document declared all lands west of the Appalachian Mountains—including the Shawnee's land in the Ohio River Valley—Indian Territory. American colonists were forbidden from settling there. But many ignored the agreement. In 1768, the Iroquois signed the Treaty of Fort Stanwix. This opened lands between the Appalachians and the Ohio River to settlement. By 1770, more than 10,000 settlers had spread across the region. In response to the influx of settlers, the Shawnee began to kidnap whites found on their lands. Some they tortured and killed, while others they adopted into the tribe.

Then, in 1774, the governor of Virginia granted land on the Ohio River to British veterans of the French and Indian War. He sent a force of 3,000 soldiers into Shawnee territory to clear the area of Indians. But the British were cut off by a surprise attack led by Shawnee chiefs Hokolesqua and **BLUE JACKET**. The resulting

Being Shawnee

DANIEL BOONE, ADOPTED SHAWNEE *In 1769, the Shawnee captured American frontiersman Daniel Boone as he hunted on their land in Kentucky. They freed him with a warning: "Go home and stay there. Don't come here anymore, for this is the Indians' hunting ground." Ignoring the warning, Boone returned to Kentucky several times. On one occasion, his eldest son was killed in a Shawnee attack. In 1778, the Shawnee captured Boone again. He was adopted into a Shawnee family but eventually escaped. Later, Boone moved to Missouri and settled for a time among the Shawnee.*

fight, which became known as the Battle of Point Pleasant, was indecisive, with equal losses on both sides. The outnumbered Shawnee were eventually forced to retreat. Afterward, the Shawnee agreed to make the Ohio River the southernmost boundary of their territory.

In 1775, the Shawnee again found themselves in the middle of a war as the **AMERICAN REVOLUTION** broke out between British forces and American colonists. The Shawnee debated whether to become involved in the war. Almost half chose to remain neutral. They moved west to Missouri to avoid the fighting. Those who remained eventually joined the fight on the side of their former enemies, the British. They felt the British had at least attempted to establish an Indian country west of the Appalachians. Americans, though, had shown they would take the land for themselves.

Throughout the war, the Shawnee destroyed settlements across the Ohio River Valley. They ambushed travelers and took many captives. In return, American forces destroyed Shawnee villages and burned their crops. Despite the Shawnee's efforts, when the war ended, they again found themselves on the losing side. The Treaty of Paris, signed in 1783, recognized American independence. It gave the newly formed United States all land east of the Mississippi, south of the Great Lakes, and north of Florida. Once again, the Shawnee had no say in the loss of their land. Many fled west across the Mississippi River. Those who remained in the Ohio River Valley continued to attack settlements. American forces kept destroying Shawnee villages as well.

In 1790, the Shawnee joined several other Indian tribes in Little Turtle's War against the U.S. In one battle, Shawnee chief Blue Jacket led a force of Indian allies against American forces led by Arthur St. Clair at Indiana's Wabash River. The Indians killed more than 600 American soldiers and wounded another 300. Only 20 Indian warriors lost their lives in the battle. The victory against St. Clair was the greatest in the history of Indian resistance to American forces.

By 1794, the Indian coalition was beginning to fall apart. In August, Blue Jacket and his forces were defeated at the Battle of Fallen Timbers in Ohio. This brought the fighting of Little Turtle's War to an end. Ninety-one chiefs from 12 Indian nations signed the Treaty of Greenville the following year, ending the war. But not all Shawnee chiefs signed the agreement. Among those who refused was a young war chief named Tecumseh, who was determined to resist American control at all costs.

The Treaty of Greenville left the Shawnee only a few small reservations in Ohio. Even these lands weren't free of the settlers who continued to flood into Ohio, which became a state in 1803. In response, many Shawnee moved west, where they felt they could better practice their traditional way of life. Most of those who remained in Ohio adopted the lifestyle of their new neighbors. They gave up hunting in favor of raising cattle and farming. They built log cabins, dressed in American-style clothing, and drank alcohol as well.

In 1805, Tecumseh's brother, Lalawethika, described a vision he'd had from the Master of Life. In Lalawethika's vision, this spirit told him Indians must turn away from white ways and return to traditional Indian customs. According to Lalawethika, the Master of Life said, "The Americans I did not make. They are not my children, but the children of the Evil Spirit." Lalawethika also claimed the Master of Life had given him special medicine, or magic, to defeat the whites and make the Shawnee invincible to bullets. After his vision, Lalawethika changed his name to Tenskwatawa, meaning "Open Door." But most whites referred to him as the Shawnee Prophet.

Tenskwatawa's message appealed to many Indians. Tecumseh helped

GENERAL ANTHONY WAYNE, WHO HAD DEFEATED
THE INDIAN COALITION AT THE BATTLE OF FALLEN
TIMBERS, NEGOTIATED THE TREATY OF GREENVILLE.

Before the War of 1812, Tecumseh traveled to Vincennes, in Indiana Territory, to speak to William Henry Harrison.

spread the message and turned it into an appeal for all Indian tribes to unite and defend remaining Indian lands against the Americans. Tecumseh believed that the land belonged to all Indians rather than to individual tribes. Therefore, he said, "No tribe has the right to sell [land], even to each other, much less to strangers. Sell a country! Why not sell the air, the great sea, as well as the earth? Did not the Great Spirit make them all for the use of his children?"

Tecumseh traveled widely, trying to convince other tribes to join his new confederation. To the Choctaw and Chickasaw, he said, "The whites are already nearly a match for us all united, and too strong for any one tribe alone to resist; so that unless we support one another with our collective and united forces ... they will soon conquer us.... Let us by unity of action destroy them all ... or drive them back whence they came."

In 1808, Tecumseh and Tenskwatawa founded a new village on the Tippecanoe River in northwestern Indiana. They named the village Prophetstown. By 1811, nearly 1,000 warriors from 30 nations, including the Ottawa, Huron, and Potawatomi, had joined Tecumseh's coalition. Even so, few Shawnee took part.

In 1811, while Tecumseh was away sharing his message, Indiana territorial governor William Henry Harrison ordered an attack on Prophetstown. Tenskwatawa heard about the impending attack and set up an ambush. But the outnumbered Indian warriors were forced to retreat, and Prophetstown was burned to the ground. The retreat signaled to many Indian nations that Tenskwatawa's medicine did not work. They gave up on Tecumseh and Tenskwatawa's coalition.

As Tecumseh prepared to regroup, America and Britain again faced off, this time in the **WAR OF 1812**. While many Shawnee

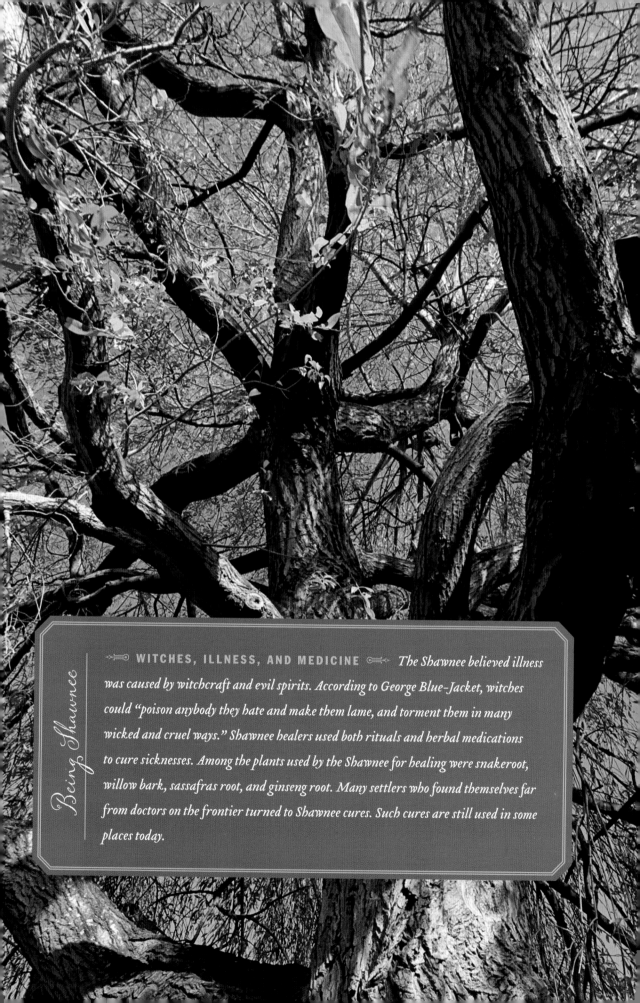

Being Shawnee

⤞ **WITCHES, ILLNESS, AND MEDICINE** ⤝ *The Shawnee believed illness was caused by witchcraft and evil spirits. According to George Blue-Jacket, witches could "poison anybody they hate and make them lame, and torment them in many wicked and cruel ways." Shawnee healers used both rituals and herbal medications to cure sicknesses. Among the plants used by the Shawnee for healing were snakeroot, willow bark, sassafras root, and ginseng root. Many settlers who found themselves far from doctors on the frontier turned to Shawnee cures. Such cures are still used in some places today.*

remained neutral and others supported the Americans, Tecumseh rallied 2,000 warriors from several tribes to fight on the side of the British. Commissioned as a brigadier general in the British army, Tecumseh led his forces to a number of victories throughout the Great Lakes region. But on October 5, 1813, Tecumseh died in the Battle of the Thames.

Tecumseh had once proclaimed, "My cause will not die, when I am dead." However, without his leadership, the Indian forces soon scattered. After the U.S. won the War of 1812, Shawnee military resistance came to an end.

War and disease had taken a toll on the Shawnee population. From 10,000 or more in the 1660s, only about 2,500 Shawnee remained by 1825. Following the War of 1812, many of the remaining Shawnee moved. Some settled in Indiana, Missouri, Kansas, Arkansas, Oklahoma, Texas, and Canada. An estimated 800 Shawnee remained in Ohio on two small reservations, where they lived much as their American neighbors. But in 1830, Congress passed the Indian Removal Act, authorizing president **ANDREW JACKSON** to move Indian tribes to lands west of the Mississippi River. By 1832, the government had taken over all Shawnee land in Ohio. The Ohio Shawnee were forced to resettle on reservations in present-day Oklahoma and Kansas.

Many Shawnee from Missouri joined the Ohio Shawnee on the Kansas reservation. Life there was better than on most reservations. The Shawnee farmed corn and oats, herded livestock, and lived in good houses. Many drove carriages and buggies. According to missionary Henry Harvey, "They live in the same manner as the whites do, and live well too." But in 1854, Kansas became a U.S. territory. Settlers descended on the region. The Shawnee reservation soon shrank from 1.6 million acres (647,497 ha) to 200,000 acres (80,937 ha).

DOZENS OF SOLDIERS TOOK CREDIT FOR KILLING TECUMSEH, INCLUDING COLONEL RICHARD MENTOR JOHNSON.

By 1869, all Shawnee had been relocated to Indian Territory. They separated into three tribes, living on different reservations: the Eastern Shawnee, Absentee Shawnee, and Loyal Shawnee. Life on Oklahoma reservations was hard. The dry soil made farming difficult. Most Shawnee became dependent on government **ANNUITIES**. In the early 1900s, many gave in to pressure from gas and oil companies to sell their land. Often, they were paid much less than the land was worth, leaving them in poverty.

Conditions among the Shawnee improved over time. Today, the various Shawnee nations are among the most prosperous American Indian communities. They remain divided into three federally recognized tribes in Oklahoma. In addition, a small number of Shawnee managed to remain in Ohio. Their descendants formed the Shawnee Nation United Remnant Band, which was recognized by the state of Ohio in 1980. Another small band—known as the Piqua Shawnee Tribe—received state recognition in

⇌ TORN BETWEEN WORLDS ⇌ *In 1879, Tecumseh's great-grandson Gaynwah enrolled in the Hampton Institute, an Indian boarding school in Virginia. The 19-year-old was sent by his tribe so that he could become a chief and help them "use the club of white man's wisdom against him in defense of our customs." But while there, Gaynwah became a Christian and took an English name, Thomas Wildcat Alford. Although he still embraced his Shawnee heritage, he was shunned upon returning to the reservation. Instead of a chief, he became a teacher.*

Alabama in 2001.

About 12,000 people of Shawnee descent live in the U.S. today. Many make a living farming, raising livestock, or working in the oil industry. Some Shawnee nations also bring in earnings from casinos, tourism, and other businesses. Such income funds healthcare, childcare, and other programs that benefit the community.

As the Shawnee have prospered, they have struggled to hold on to their culture. The Shawnee language is today considered endangered. However, by offering classes in the language, the Shawnee are taking strides to prevent it from disappearing. Many Shawnee also continue to observe traditional ceremonies. But convincing young people to participate in such ceremonies can prove difficult. As chief Andy Warrior said, "We have to compete with these cars, these video games, … air conditioning." Still, Warrior knows that taking part in these traditions is a way of keeping the tribe's culture alive. The Shawnee have faced many changes throughout their history, from their first encounters with Europeans to their attempt to unite Indian nations to fight off encroaching settlers. Through it all, the Shawnee have retained their identity while adapting to the changing world around them.

SHAWNEE POWWOWS TODAY OFTEN FEATURE ARTWORK, TRADITIONAL OUTFITS, CEREMONIAL DANCES, AND DRUMMING.

Shawnee elders often spent an entire day or night telling stories to the younger generations. Their stories provided younger members of the tribe with practical guidance for war and everyday life. They also taught Shawnee values such as bravery and loyalty and passed on Shawnee traditions and beliefs. In many stories, such as this one, people could become animals and vice versa.

One day, a young warrior named Red Hawk traveled farther into the forest than anyone had ever gone. There he found a meadow. In the center of the meadow was a circular path. But no tracks led to or from the path. Red Hawk looked all around to figure out who could have made such a path, but he saw nothing.

So Red Hawk hid in the trees and watched the meadow. As he waited, a large basket floated down from the sky. It held several young sky maidens. The women hopped out of the basket and danced on the circular path. Red Hawk thought Morning Star, the youngest of the maidens, was the most beautiful. He ran to her and grabbed her hand. But the maidens jumped back into the basket in fear and disappeared into the sky.

The next day, Red Hawk changed himself into a woodchuck. He hid near the path, and when the maidens again came down, he watched them dance. But when Morning Star saw him, she cried out in fear, and the women again floated back into the sky.

Red Hawk knew he couldn't give up. The next day, he changed himself into a mouse and waited at the edge of the meadow. This time, when the women came down, Morning Star held out her hand for the cute mouse to climb into it. When she touched the mouse, Red Hawk changed into himself. The other women were afraid and disappeared, but Morning Star remained with Red Hawk and married him. They had a baby boy and were happy.

After a while, Morning Star missed her family. One day, while Red Hawk was hunting, Morning Star climbed into a basket with her son, and they traveled to the sky. On Earth, Red Hawk was devastated. Years went by, but still he spent much time near the circle, hoping his wife and child would return.

Meanwhile, in the sky, Morning Star's son missed his father. Finally, the boy's grandfather told Morning Star to go back to Earth to get Red Hawk. So she and the boy jumped in the basket and returned to Red Hawk, who was overjoyed to see them again.

Morning Star instructed Red Hawk to hunt for one of each kind of bird and animal. Then she brought him to the sky, along with a small part from each animal. When they reached the stars, Red Hawk handed the animal parts out to all the sky people. The people turned into the animals and went to Earth to fill the forests. Red Hawk, Morning Star, and their son each chose a hawk feather. They all turned into hawks and returned to Earth, where they still soar above the forests and meadows today.

AMERICAN REVOLUTION
(1775–83) the war in which 13 British colonies in North America fought Britain for independence

ANDREW JACKSON
(1767–1845) army general who fought many successful battles against Indian tribes and in 1829 became the country's seventh president; he signed the Indian Removal Act, which relocated Indians to lands west of the Mississippi River

ANNUITIES
monies paid on a regular basis; the U.S. government often offered Indian nations annuities when they moved onto reservations

ANTHROPOLOGISTS
people who study the physical traits, cultures, and relationships of different peoples

BLUE JACKET
(c. 1740–1805) Shawnee chief who led resistance to American settlement on Shawnee lands but accepted some white customs, living in an American-style home, marrying a French-Shawnee woman, and sending his son to be educated in Detroit

CONFEDERACY
a group of nations or states that join together for a specific purpose

CONSENSUS
agreement by all or most of a group

CRADLEBOARD
a board or frame to which an infant could be strapped to be carried on the back

FASTED
went without eating, often as part of a religious ritual

FRENCH AND INDIAN WAR
(1754–63) conflict between Britain and France over control of North America

NOMADIC
moving from place to place rather than living in a permanent home

SCALPS
portions of the skin at the top of the head, with the attached hair, that were sometimes cut off of enemies as battle trophies or to claim a reward

SHAMAN
a spiritual leader often believed to have healing and other powers

TRAVOIS
a vehicle made of two poles crossed into a V-shape at one end, with a bison hide hung between them to serve as a platform; the travois was hitched to a dog or horse, with the ends dragging on the ground

WAR OF 1812
(1812–15) conflict between the U.S. and Britain over trade restrictions and Indian land rights

WILLIAM HENRY HARRISON
(1773–1841) U.S. territorial governor of Indiana who led campaigns against the Shawnee and other Indians; his defeat of Tecumseh at Prophetstown on the Tippecanoe River helped him win the 1840 presidential election, but he died after only one month in office

Callender, Charles. "Shawnee," in *Northeast*, ed. Bruce G. Trigger. Vol. 15 of *Handbook of North American Indians*. Ed. William C. Sturtevant. Washington, D.C.: Smithsonian, 1978.

Calloway, Colin G. *The Shawnees and the War for America*. New York: Viking, 2007.

Cassidy, James J., ed. *Through Indian Eyes: The Untold Story of Native American Peoples*. Pleasantville, N.Y.: Reader's Digest, 1995.

Clark, Jerry E. *The Shawnee*. Lexington: University Press of Kentucky, 1993.

Gilbert, Bil. *God Gave Us This Country: Tekamthi and the First American Civil War*. New York: Atheneum, 1989.

Miller, Lee, ed. *From the Heart: Voices of the American Indian*. New York: Knopf, 1995.

Sugden, John. *Tecumseh: A Life*. New York: Henry Holt, 1998.

Warren, Stephen. *The Worlds the Shawnees Made: Migration and Violence in Early America*. Chapel Hill: University of North Carolina Press, 2014.

⊶⊷ READ MORE ⊶⊷

Collinson, Clare, ed. *Peoples of the East, Southeast, and Plains*. Redding, Conn.: Brown Bear Books, 2009.

Wilds, Mary C. *The Shawnee*. San Diego: Lucent Books, 2003.

⊶⊷ WEBSITES ⊶⊷

EASTERN SHAWNEE TRIBE OF OKLAHOMA: SHAWNEE LANGUAGE
https://www.estoo-nsn.gov/culture /shawnee-language/
Learn Shawnee greetings, animal names, and numbers, and try a Shawnee language word search.

OHIO HISTORY CENTRAL: SHAWNEE INDIANS
http://www.ohiohistorycentral.org/w /Shawnee_Indians
Learn more about Shawnee history in Ohio, including information on battles and important leaders.